Dedication

I would like to dedicate this book to my children, Craig J.A. Erskine, Jeremiah M. Erskine and Jahmilah 'Queen' K. Erskine. My children are my most cherished creations. They have taught me so much. They have given me unconditional love and it is because of them that I dare say "I know what Love is". They accept me with all my flaws and love me still. They have forgiven all my mistakes and love me still. Each so unique and yet the same in their love for me. I have never claimed to be the perfect mother, I wanted only to give my children that which I felt I lacked. I do my best and still make mistakes. They continue to forgive, accept, and love. My oldest son Craig, always asked me 'Mom what does God look like? Where did he come from? Who made him?' Well my Prince I do not know the Source of the Creators of Us. But What I have found out who the creators of Us are. Perhaps you will continue the search and answer that question for future generations.

About the Author:

Aye, formerly known as Andrea Della Pettway, is a prolific writer and busy mother of three. The daughter of an adventurous mother who enlisted in the U.S. Army, when Aye was 8 years old .Born in Detroit, Michigan November 26, 1969, and was raised in New Jersey, California, Florida and Berlin Germany. Aye had an older sister, Samia, she passed away in Berlin, Germany October 2006. In 1986 Aye moved to Los Angeles California and lived with her aunt. After graduating from Washington Preparatory High School, Aye joined the armed forces and was stationed in Germany.

After leaving the army where she met her husband, Craig Erskine, she settled into married life and motherhood. Aye has always enjoyed writing her thoughts down and while living in Columbus, Georgia Aye began develop her own style of poetry. In the midst of raising children, managing a home and coping with life's challenges, she managed to create an impressive body of work.

In 1996 Aye's mother passed away in Germany, having never seen her grandchildren. Her mother's death served as a catalyst for Aye. She began in earnest to achieve her goal in writing. She designed, produced and marketed posters and art that showcased her poems. She has self published two books of poetry titled I Am Aye and Visions in Aye's Heart. Aye now lives in Columbus, Georgia with her children.

Our Divine Story

A story within HisStory

Forealsister Designs

1448 Kevin Court

Columbus, GA 31907

www.Forealsister.webs.com

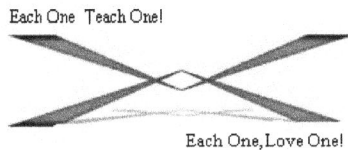

ISBN-13: 978-0615844947
ISBN-10: 0615844944
Cover Designed by Jeremiah M. Erskine

First published by Forealsister Designs on 07.11.2013

Printed in the United States of America.

This book is printed on acid-free paper.

ForealSister

Designs

Each One Teach One!

Each One, Love One!

TABLE OF CONTENTS

Introduction:

Inspired by the condition of our planet and the limited supply of true history, I decided to write a book for your consideration. So much of Our Divine Story has been lost, destroyed, stolen and re written, motivated by man's desires for world domination. Misinformation has caused severe damage to Human Spiritual Awareness. I feel the need to help inform the Human Race of the misrepresentation of Our Divine Story. In hopes of not separating the black story from the white story, or the religious story from the world story, so that the next generations will have the courage, wisdom and knowledge to bring about a New Story, the Human Story. According to accepted, known history, it is unknown how life on this planet began. The origins of life are in constant debate, evolution, or Divine creation? I venture to say that Human life on this planet began as a result of the combination of the two. At this point I feel the need to express that I am not educated beyond some college courses. I hold no educational degrees except for vocational school. I am not an academic. What I think I know, I have learned through independent study. I will write in common English so that what I say can be Over Stood by All. Verification for all that I say in this book is nothing new. It can be found through research. The story of Genesis in the Bible came from a much older story. It is a story that was originally written in an alien language called Cuneiform, on clay tablets. I will not be giving point by point details. I just want to point out some of the 'great mysteries' in the bible and show you how man has taken your Divine Story and turned it into His story. I don't expect you to believe any of what I say. I do however expect that if any of what you read here makes just a little bit of sense. Ask a question, search for the answers. I intend to provide my main references to help get you started on your search for truth if it is important to you to know who you are and from where you came. Make your own determinations. I will not censor my thoughts or my beliefs. You can either agree of disagree, the choice is yours. From the beginning of our education we have been taught lies. They have lied to us about our very Creator. I am no Scientist, so I will not say that I know how the Universe was formed or how the first single celled organisms found their way onto this planet. What I do know is that once on Earth those organisms evolved. Here I feel the need to let you know that I believe The One True Creator, 'God' to be the Grand Architect of Science. So you can not separate God from science, which man has attempted to do. They are one in the same.

Most of the information contained in the bible was taken from Ancient Sumerian and Aramaic Text. The Bible is what I call a watered down version of Our Divine Story. The tales of ancient myths and legends is where most of our true history lies. Why else would it survive? I love the way they put the truth right in your face and call it science fiction, myth, or legend

The Gods:

The Main characters in Our Divine Story were in ancient days referred to as The Anunnaki, (those who from above came down) also commonly known as The Gods.

These are the main Characters:

Nammu, Goddess of the Primeval Sea, "the mother who gave birth to heaven and earth."

An, God of the Heavens, King on Nibiru.

Antu, official spouse of An.

Enlil, God of Air and Storms, second born son of An, legal successor to the throne. Enlil is supreme ruler of Sumerian pantheon of gods on Earth.

Ea, Lord of Water and Wisdom, First born son of An, second in line for the throne.

Ninmah, Mother Earth, the source of all life, daughter of An.

Ninurta, Enlil's foremost son, not born by legal spouse but by Enlil's half sister Ninmah.

Marduk, Ea's foremost son and legal successor.

Dummuzi, Ea's youngest son,

Utu, the god of justice, Enlil's grandson and Inanna's twin brother.

Inanna, Goddess of Love and War, Enlil's granddaughter and Utu's twin sister

Ereshkigal, Goddess of Darkness, Gloom, and Death, sister of Inanna

Enlil, Military
Commander

Ea aka Enki,
Master of the Water.
The Artful Fashioner,
One of Our Creators

Enlil's Bull

Ninurta, Enlil and Ninmah's Son

Inanna, Goddess of War and Love
Enlil's Granddaughter

Over the years and across the regions, the names and aspects of the gods were sometimes interchanged. Depending on who was writing the story, as it has always been who did what depends on the pen holder's perspective. One story depicts Enlil as the 'evil' one.

And of course there is another that depicts Ea and definitely his son Marduk as the 'evil' one. And of course let's not forget the story that depicts Inanna and the entire race of women as the 'evil' one. They all tell the same story, just from the perspective they want

the reader to see. The story that I intend to tell is from a combination of Ea's and Inanna's perspective. These were Human beings from a different planet, the same as us genetically. If you ask me they are all responsible for the 'evil' that exist in our world today. From these people we developed our civilization. The Human ego can be a powerful and dangerous force. Religion and war have forged our civilization, deception being the primary weapon used. It will destroy our civilization as well. The stage is set.

Our Ancient ancestors set it long ago. Only the truth will help mankind understand why the wars must end. If we should continue to war with each other we should at least know the truth about how and why we are fighting ancient wars. The blood that has been shed in the name of one belief or another should sicken us. If you want to know the truth of it all, you must ask a question and search for the answer. Read, and re read, and re read!!! There is only one Truth, it may be colored all shades of the rainbow. But when the color fades, the truth remains. For those of you who do not wish to believe that the god you worship is not actually a god at all, you will dismiss all of what I say. But overstand that I am no atheist, because of my love for God I was lead to seek out side of the religious

world for answers that made sense to me. Religious doctrine seeks to keep God a mystery that only religion can decipher. God does not want us to worship in ignorance. In fact The One True Creator of All does not want, has not requested, or need our worship. The Creators of Us required that we worship and serve them. That is why we were created, it was our purpose. In order to free ourselves from the need to worship, we need accurate knowledge of The True Creator so that we may know self. Instead of feeding our spiritual

man has used religion to exploit it. Making demands on you that God knows you can not live up to yet especially since you have not been given accurate knowledge of your history. Not wanting to tell you the truth of who you are, they tell you to walk in faith. I say faith has it's place for those who are content to remain ignorant. I choose to walk in knowledge. I don't claim to know it all. I am wise enough to know this; the man who knows anything, knows that he knows nothing at all. You can spend an entire lifetime studying a single blade of grass and never know all there is to know about that single blade of grass. From the very first paragraph it will read like science fiction. But let's take a look at science fiction. Is it life imitating art or art imitating life? Thirty years ago I can remember watching Star Trek on TV, intergalactic travel and communication, using computers, cell phones and IPads, then. 'Beam me up Scottie', who knew GE has teleportation technology patented? Frankenstein, the ability of creating a creature out of flesh and bone but not of spirit. Immaculate Conception, giving birth with out having known a man. All science fiction thirty years ago and reality today. To think that man evolved from a primate into the technology advanced society that were are today in mere thousands of years is arrogant to say the least. As you read my version to Our Divine Story I ask that you open your mind to the possibilities. I know it will be hard for many of you to accept any of what I say as truth.

My intentions are to share a well known story and reveal a well hidden story within that story. Join Aye on a journey to Our past so that we can Overstand Our Present and hopefully better Our Future.

Chapter One Mission Earth

According Ancient Sumerian Text, and I am paraphrasing here, Life on this planet began when another planet (Nibiru) that enters our orbit system approximately every 36,000 years collided with our planet. It was the collision of this planet with our planet which at that time was known as Taimat, (Watery One), which planted the Seed of Life. It was also this collision that is responsible for creating our Moon and the Milky Way (known in ancient times as The Hammered Belt).Now according to the same Sumerian Text, on the planet Nibiru Human Life was already in existence. As to be expected, where there are Humans there is bond to be conflict. So on Nibiru all the tribes gathered into two great nations, the nations of the South against the nations of the North. A war broke out between the two nations and lasted for many years. After much desolation and lost life a truce was declared. North and South became One Nation under One King's reign. North and South were by marriage United. The first born son would be the successor to the Throne, and thus a dynasty was formed there by establishing unity on Nibiru forever.

Forever was short lived when another rivalry occurred. A treasonous member of the royal court (Alalu) killed the king and placed himself upon the throne and pronounced himself king. His entitlement was questioned, and unity in the land was lost. The actual heir to the throne (Anu) challenged Alalu, to hand to hand combat. Anu was victorious in the battle. Alalu fled. Alalu now defeated by Anu decides to take a spacecraft and attempts to make the trip to Earth, beyond the Hammered Belt in search of the precious metal needed on Nibiru to repair the breach in the planet's atmosphere. If he survived the journey, and found the precious metals needed he would hold the fate of Nibiru in his hands and they would have to allow him the Kingship. Traveling thru the Hammered Bracelet was difficult, he used weapons of terror to blast thru. His journey was successful. His spacecraft crashed in the oceans of South East Africa. There in the ocean, he found the much needed precious mental that he sought. Alalu then communicates with King Anu, that he is on a new world and has found the Gold needed to repair Nibiru's atmosphere. He demands that King Anu submit to his conditions and hand over the Kingship. The King calls the counsel and they decide to send the king's eldest son, Ea (second in line to the throne because his mother was not the legal spouse of Anu, she was a concubine), to Earth to verify Alalu's claims. If his claims are true the king will once again engage in hand to hand combat with Alalu for the throne of Nibiru. Ea travels to Earth with fifty soldiers and his ship's commander. To pass thru the Hammered Bracelet Ea used Water instead of weapons. Once on Earth Ea begins the seven days of creation, one day on Nibiru is equal to one thousand years on Earth. Those seven days consisted of creating damns, separating the rivers from the oceans, identifying trees, plants, animals, birds, the creatures in the sea, and building living quarters. On the seventh day they rested. *The creation process actually took seven thousand years. Earth Humans were not created until thousands of years later.* Ea verifies Alalu's claims that the gold required to repair the atmosphere on Nibiru is indeed on Earth. They begin to attempt to retrieve the gold from the oceans but it is not enough. For many years they toiled to locate the source of the gold veins on Earth that the ancient legends spoke of. The king and the nation grow inpatient with the slow progress of obtaining the gold. The king orders Ea to repair Alalu's spacecraft and return what ever gold they have collected back to Nibiru to see if this metal will repair the atmosphere. Ea gathered and separated all of the metals he had collected to send back to Nibiru. Abgal travels back to Nibiru with the samples that Ea provided. The gold is refined into dust and tested. It is indeed able to repair the atmosphere on Nibiru! In the meantime on Earth Ea had discovered the Earth's golden veins in South Africa and communicated this information back to Nibiru. But obtaining the gold from the Earth veins was a difficult task. A plan was devised by Anu's youngest son, Enlil. It was then decided that Enlil, (Ea's younger brother and next in line for the throne because he is the first born son of Anu's legal spouse) would travel to Earth and implement his plan and to be put in charge of the Earth Mission. Once on Earth Enlil decided to send for more soldiers and build more settlements and assign leaders over each settlement. King Anu then came to Earth and engaged in hand to hand combat with Alalu and once again King Anu was victorious. The fallen Alalu pulled the king to the ground and bit off and swallowed his phallus. For his crime of ending the king's ability to procreate, Alalu was sentenced to die in exile on the planet Mars. The face on Mars is his tomb. Anzu volunteers to stay on Mars with Alalu until he dies. King Anu returns and remains King on Nibiru. Before Anu returned to Nibiru, the king holds a council with the Anunnaki leaders to assign duties. Ea requested to be assigned commander of The Edin since it was he who has established it and his brother in charge of the gold extraction. Enlil disagreed, he felt that he was the better commander, and since The Landing Place was located in The Edin, he should be assigned commander of The Edin. Ea had knowledge of the secretes of The Earth, he had discovered Earth's golden veins in South Africa and therefore he should be assigned the task of obtaining the gold. Anu listened to his son's angry words and considered returning one of them to Nibiru. He decided to draw by lots and let fate decide who would return to Nibiru, who would command The Edin and who would perform the gold extraction in South Africa. Ea was assigned the region of South Africa, the seas and the oceans. Enlil was assigned the Edin, southern Mesopotamia. (Modern day Iraq) The Mission Control Center was also located in Mesopotamia. The Landing Place was built in Mesopotamia as well for the purpose of shipping raw materials back to Nibiru. Way stations were built on Mars and Venus and soldiers were assigned to them. Anzu was assigned the duty of the first commander of the Way Stations. It was he who stayed on Mars with Alalu while he awaited his death.

(War over oil and regional stability? I think not! This war is about extraterrestrials, ancient birth rights, ancient space ports and real

live star gates.) I think Anu should have taken one of the brothers back with him. By choosing to allow both of them to remain, he sealed the fate of this planet. These two brothers rarely agreed on anything.

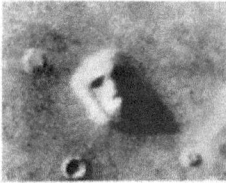

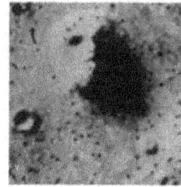

The Face on Mars, Alanu's Tomb

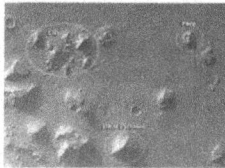

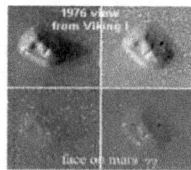

Possible Star Gate Locations

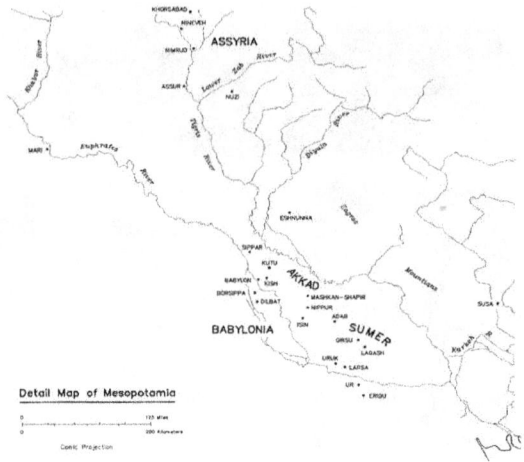

Detail Map of Mesopotamia

Ancient Sumer, Enlil's Domain. City of the Gods, Also where Inanna's royal city was built.

The next to arrive on Earth was Ninmah, the sister of Ea and Enlil, and the first born daughter of the king. All three shared one father, the king, but three different mothers. With Ninmah came fifty chosen females, and seeds of Nibiru to be sewn on Earth. Ninmah was a chief medical officer and these fifty chosen women were healers. Ninmah's Healing City and her abode was located in Mesopotamia. On her way to Earth she stopped on Mars to find that Alalu and Anzu had died. Ninmah gave to Anzu the waters of Life and he was resurrected. Anzu showed her the cave in which he had left Alalu's dead body. It sat upon a mountain in which they engraved the image of Alalu's face, looking toward Nibiru. She left twenty soldiers on Mars with Anzu and continued to travel to Earth. Ea has developed tools for digging and extracting the gold from beneath the surface of the Earth. Tunnels were fashioned and mines were built. Because of the harsh conditions of working the mines, the soldiers were having a difficult time adjusting to Earth's thin atmosphere, the heat of South Africa, and receiving little rest, mutiny erupted. It was at this time when it was decided to create a primitive worker to ease the toil of the Anunnaki soldiers working in the gold mines in South Africa. *But still it was many years yet before our ancestors, Adam and Eve came to be.* This idea was primarily conceived by Ea and performed by Ninmah and Ea's son Ningishzidda, but all three of the primary leaders of the Earth Mission agreed to create a primitive worker to ease the toil of the soldiers. *(hence the statement in the bible… 'let Us create a man…')* *In the bible whenever the text refers to God, it is one of these three,*

Enlil, Ea, and Ninmah, and at times Enlil's son Ninurta and his granddaughter Inanna. I call the three main characters the Trinity. If you have ever read the bible and wondered why God's personality seemed to change..... there you go. There were three main characters. Man took these three very different individuals and combined them into one singular male god. The first Earth humanoid was a little more evolved than primates. The actual creator of the primitive Earth Human was Ninmah, and one of Ea's sons, Ningishzidda. This was accomplished by genetic manipulation and the combining of her DNA with that of the primate already in existence on Earth. It was trial and error until finally they were successful. *(The Island of Dr Moreau)* The purpose for the creation of Earth Human was for the humans to procreate and produce workers to take over the toil in the mines. *'Be fruitful and multiply'* Enlil was angered because they had given the Earth Human knowledge of procreation and feared that Ea and Ninmah had also bestowed upon the Earth Humans the essence of the Anunnaki's long life. Ninmah assured Enlil that essence of longevity was not given to the Earth Humans. Angered by the actions of his siblings Enlil ordered the first Earth Humanoids out of the Edin and banished them to South Africa. There they began breeding and began the first Earth Humanoid populace. It was the inter breeding between Ea and two different Earth Humans many years later that resulted in our ancestors, Adam and Eve. These Two were more liken to their creators than the previous primitive worker. Adam and Eve were intelligent. They were removed from South Africa and taken to the

Edin to live and learn among the Anunnaki. Ea did not disclose to his brother and sister that he was the father of Adam and Eve. But when the King requested that Adam be sent to Nibiru for consideration and examination, he sent word to his father that he was indeed the father of Adam and Eve. *(So here we learn that Adam was the first Earth Human to travel out to space. Esua? Also that his mother and father were of flesh, bone, and spirit.)* Civilized Earth Human has been created. On Nibiru, Anu is quite taken with the mini version of the Anunnaki. His son had on a new world a new being created! Adam remained on Nibiru for a year. The king gave his approval and sent Adam back to Earth with instructions that his education should continue. *Adam's bloodline would be the first Earth Human Royal Bloodline. This is how we came to be. Not by some mysterious breath, being, and man not yet come to be. But, how about mud was used in the creation of Us? It is important to state here that the Anunnaki did not view them selves as GOD. They are very much aware of a Supreme Divine Creator of All That Is. But because of what appeared to mere Earth Human, as their Immortality, vast knowledge of technology, the fact that the Anunnaki created them, and their ability to navigate the solar system, they were viewed as Gods. This came in handy when religion was born.* When it was decided to create the Primitive Earth Human, of the Trinity, only one stood in objection, Enlil. It is an abomination he declared! He thought that by manipulating genetics to create a new species was like playing GOD. Ninmah argued that the Divine Creator saw fit to bestow such knowledge to them, why then if not for this purpose? Fate or Destiny? This is the question that the Anunnaki pondered. In the end he agreed to create the Primitive Worker with the condition that once the gold was obtained, they would be left to die when the Anunnaki returned to Nibiru. *This is when Slavery on this Planet began. They were in fact playing God, and have been trying to clear their Karmic Debt ever since. Much of the condition of our current world can be blamed on the examples that they set. In their image, they made us. The apple doesn't fall far from the tree.*

Possibly Ancient Ruins of Ea's Palace in Ethiopia

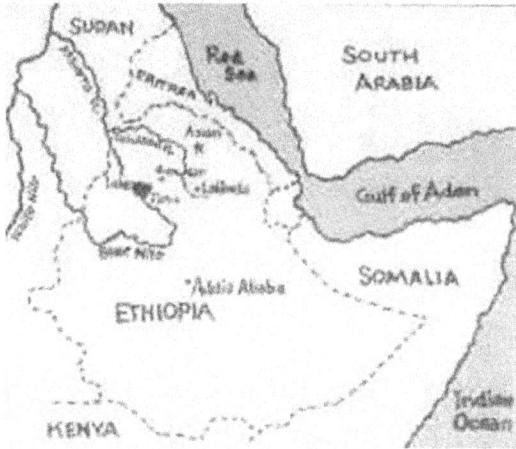

Nubian Map, Ea's Domain

Chapter: Two Marduk

Another central character that we must talk about is Marduk. Marduk is the Son of Ea and Ea's legal spouse Ninki. Marduk and Ninki are summoned to Earth by Ea sometime after Anu returns to Nibiru. After which Enlil and Ninmah send for their son, Ninurta. There by intensifying the already set stage for war on Earth. In the Bible Marduk is none other than the one they call Satan, The Evil One. Now as a human being I can empathize with his complaints, not all of his actions. All that is blamed on Satan in the Bible is not true. Just as they changed the three central individuals into one God, they blamed every evil act of which ever leader committed squarely on Marduk or women. (What I find funny is how they say that Satan is jealous of Us and our relationship with God. Ha! Nothing could be farther from the truth. He forsakes his Princely Rights on Nibiru, and took for his Legal Spouse an Earth Human. In doing so he was told that he would never be able to return to Nibiru.)

Marduk's father, Ea, first born to the king, not by legal spouse but by concubine. Ninmah, first born daughter to the king was also conceived by a concubine. Enlil is the second born son but by the legal spouse of the king and thereby legal heir to the throne. Marduk felt that it was his father's birthright as first born son of the king to be next in line for the throne. Since it was his father who came to Earth and started the Earth Mission, he felt his father should be allowed to rule the Earth and the new beings that he and his aunt had created. Instead the king had put Enlil in charge of the Earth

Mission. Enlil assigns Marduk as the Commander of the soldiers on Mars and his son, Ninurta commander of the Landing Place. Ea, who feels slighted as well, promises Marduk Supremacy on Earth. The Anunnaki were also proliferating on Earth. It would not be long before rivalries between clans broke out on Earth. Now on Earth there are two Anunanki Clans, Ea's Clan and Enlil's Clan. Some born on Earth some born on Nibiru. Enlil was married on Earth after he raped a young priestess and she became pregnant. Their son was the first of the Anunnaki to be born on Earth. His name was Ishkur. It is important to point out here that Ninmah as half sister to both bothers and the first born daughter of the king she was betrothed to her brother Ea. But she was in love with Enlil. He seduced her and she bore him a child, Ninurta. The king did not approve of her actions and decreed that she would never be allowed to marry. (Ninurta was born on Nibiru as was Marduk.) Marduk's mother, a Princess was espoused to Ea after Ninmah's indiscretion. Marduk was a legal heir, but Ninurta was not because his parents were not married, but by the double seed factor if rights to the throne ever became an issue between Ninurta and Marduk, Ninurta would inherit the throne. Ninmah also bore Ea many daughters but Ea desired a son. He desired a son from his sister because if he had a son with her, by the double seed factor their son would have entitlements to the throne. When Adam and Eve had children, they were named Kain and Abel. Marduk was impressed by their parents, Adam and Eve and enjoyed the company of the boys, he was after all their uncle.

Marduk suggests that he be the mentor of one of the boys, and Enlil's son, Ninurta mentor the other. Ninurta took Kain to the Metal City where they smelted and refined the gold. There he was taught the art of agriculture. Abel was taken to the meadows where he was taught shepherding. Dumizi, Marduk's younger brother, on Earth born went to Nibiru and returned with four legged animals. Sheep, Lambs, and goats. *We all know the story of Kain and Abel. It was not Kain's intention to kill his brother. He had no idea when he struck his brother that the blow would end his life. Take a look at the reason, they were competing for the affections of the Gods. What we didn't know is that murder intensified family rivalries on Earth.* For the crime of slaying his brother Kain was exiled from The Edin, away from civilized man and the Anunnaki. Marduk was very angry and not satisfied with the punishment. For the crime of killing his brother Marduk felt that Kain should be put to death. At this time Ea decided to tell Marduk the truth about the parentage of Adam and Eve and how Kain and Abel were in fact his nephews. Surprised at first, and then amused by his father's sexual prowess. Marduk agrees to allow Kain to live but to the ends of the Earth he and his household will be banished, deprived of his birthright, but from his seed seven nations will be born. *(The mark that was placed on Kain was the inability to produce facial hair. He was unable to grow a beard.) This incident also served as another thorn in Marduk's side because he felt that Enlil was favoring Ninurta by not sentencing Kain to death.* After this incident the Anunnaki gave Adam and Eve permission to proliferate. So began the Genesis of Adam and Eve,

Our Divine Ancestors.

In the days of Noah, there were many hardships on Earth and Mars. On Earth and Mars atmospheric changes were occurring. Nibiru's 36,000 year circuit was entering our solar system, causing the atmospheric changes. On Mars dryness and dust was enveloping the planet. On Earth climate changes were occurring. The ice caps in Antarctica were melting. Summers were hotter, the winters colder, volcanic eruptions and earth quakes were occurring. *Sounds like what is going on today.* It was at that time that Marduk decided to take a bride. Ea was happy to hear that his son wished to be married until Marduk informed him that it was a Daughter of Adam, not Nibiru that he wished to marry. To marry an Earthling was unheard of for a Prince of Nibiru! All of his princely rights on Nibiru would be forsaken and he nor his spouse and offspring would ever be allowed to return to Nibiru. Marduk felt that his 'princely rights' were non existent, trampled on as were his father's. After discussing the matter with Ninki, it was decided to allow Marduk to marry the daughter of Adam. Enlil of course objected to the marriage and bought the matter to King Anu. The King consulted the counselors on Nibiru. There were no laws in place to address the marriage of an Anunnaki and Earthling. It was decided that Marduk should be allowed to marry, but to Nibiru he could never return. Enlil accepted the King's word and informed Marduk that he had the blessing of the king but that he and his wife could not remain in the Edin. Marduk and his bride would be assigned a domain of their own as a wedding gift. The soldiers on Mars heard of their commander's espousal, Shamgaz, the surrogate commander for Marduk suggested that they would go to Earth and take for themselves brides. Why should they remain on Mars with out spouse or offspring? If their commander was allowed to take an Earthling for a bride they would as well. They devised a plan to abduct the Earth Women when they went to Earth for the wedding. *This is when the sons of god took the daughters of man that is stated in the bible, and would become known as the rebellious ones, rebels.* Of the three hundred soldiers stationed on Mars two hundred came to Earth to attend Marduk's wedding with the intention of abducting daughters of Adam to take as wives so they too could proliferate. Marduk's wedding celebration was more like a king's coronation than a wedding. During the festivities, the Rebels abducted the daughters of Adam. Shamgaz announced to the Anunnaki leaders that they intended to take the women back to Mars so they too could proliferate. The leaders summoned Marduk and told him to take control of the situation. Marduk agreed with the rebels and defended their right to marry. Ea and Ninki reluctantly agreed. Enlil considered it yet another evil deed and his anger could not be pacified. He agreed to allow the rebels their women, but let them return to Mars, on Earth they can not remain! The conditions on Mars had become unbearable and the rebels could no longer survive the atmospheric changes on Mars. So the soldiers must remain on Earth. Enlil declared that in the Edin they could not remain so to Marduk's domain many of the rebels settled.

Here I would like to point out that it was Enlil, not Marduk who sought to destroy the Earthling and all offspring between the Anunnaki and the Earthling. Enlil saw mankind as an abomination and now the Anunnaki were breeding them, an even greater abomination. As a result of his marriage to Sarpanit many Earthling were loyal to Marduk. Enlil and his son Ninurta took notice to Marduk's increasing strength. Fearful that Marduk and his Earthlings would take over ruler ship of the Earth they devised a plan to reduce the Earthling population by reducing the food rations.

Machu Picchu

The Nazca Lines

tiahuanaco-man

Stone Heads - Tiahuanaco

Located in Inanna's Domain, Peru

Elponce

Tia-Gate

Chapter Three: Noah

Noah came to be because Ea raped his mother who was married to one of the Anunnaki. When Noah was born he was of white skin and his eyes were blue. Noah's father suspected that one of the rebels was the actual father of Noah because of his odd appearance. He questioned Noah's mother about the child and she denied that she had been with one of the rebels. But she did not disclose that Ea was the actual father of her child. The Anunnaki were greatly puzzled by his appearance but soon came to adore Noah and taught him many things. He grew up, was espoused and had three sons. Suffering on Earth at that time was great. Earthlings were over taken with disease and pestilence. Ninmah wished to teach the Earthling the Art of practicing medicine so that they could cure themselves and prevent more disease outbreaks. Enlil forbade Ninmah from teaching the Earthlings curing. Ea wished to teach them how to build canals so that they could obtain sustenance from the fish of the sea. This too Enlil forbade. Enlil wished to see the Earthling perish by disease and pestilence. The Anunnaki were also suffering due to the gravity changes in the solar system which caused harsh climatic changes on Earth and Mars. Their rations were also in low supply. The nearing of Nibiru and his great gravitational pull was causing the changes. When it got closest to Earth the ice caps in the artic would fall and cause a watery calamity. The Anunnaki of Earth began preparing for the great calamity. The Earth would be evacuated to Mars to wait out the calamity. The gold mines were shut down, as well as the refining plants. At that time a mysterious guest arrived on Earth with a message from King Anu, he announced to Enlil. 'I am Galzu, emissary plenipotentiary King and Council'. Enlil summoned Ea and Ninmah. Once the Trinity assembled, Galzu informed them that they were not able to return to Nibiru because of the lengthy amount of time they had spent on Earth their life cycles had adjusted to Earth. Should they return to Nibiru they would die. The Trinity was deeply sadden to hear this, on Earth they had become old and appeared to be twice their age. Galzu also informed them that they should wait out the calamity in spacecrafts, because conditions on Mars had become unpredictable. For those who were able and wished to return to Nibiru would be allowed to return home. No Earthling, Marduk's wife included would be allowed to return to Nibiru. The Trinity informed the Anunnaki leaders of their choices to wait out the calamity in aerial ships or return to Nibiru. They were also informed that the Earthlings would be left to perish. Enlil required all leaders to take an oath of silence. Ninmah was reluctant to take the oath, she had created them, and they were her children and cared a great deal for the Earthlings. But she did take the oath. Ea and Marduk however refused to take the oath. Now on Earth the Anunnaki are preparing to either return to Nibiru, evacuate to spacecraft, or relocate to the mountains. Ea and Ninmah decide that once the calamity hits Earth all of their work would have been in vain unless they preserved the life essence of all that they had created. They collected all of the life essence on Earth, both female and male, two by two. Historical records were also carefully recorded and buried so that future generations would know all the history of the Earth.

Prior to the great flood Ea had a dream vision in which the King's emissary Galzu, appeared and informed Ea that the Earthlings shall inherit the Earth. He then instructed Ea to summon his son Noah and without breaking the oath inform him of the coming calamity. He also told him to tell Noah to build a submarine so that his family and the seed of all that is useful be it plant or animal would be preserved. 'So is the will of the Creator of All'. *Notice here that the king's emissary does not say it is a command from the king, but a command from 'The Creator Of All'! Acknowledging that the Anunnaki were aware of a Universal Creator of All. Apparently they have not at this point in history been in His presence either. There could be millions of planets out there with intelligent life. So now The One True Creator steps in for the first time on the Earth Human's behalf. Stating that we shall inherit the Earth and commands that all useful life on Earth shall be preserved. There is but One God. They were well aware of this when they decided to portray themselves to us as gods. Committing what I think the church calls Blasphemy. Or is it Heresy? What ever the crime they killed Jesus for. Talk about hypocrisy.*

When Ea awoke he sent his emissary to locate Galzu.

After searching for Galzu to no avail his emissary informed him that Galzu had returned to Nibiru long ago. That night to Noah's reed hut he went, speaking to Noah's wall so as to not break the oath, he told the wall of the coming calamity and what must be done to preserve

Noah's family's life. He left at the door of the reed hut a tablet with the instructions for building the submarine. A final warning to the wall he gave, the purpose of the submarine was to remain secrete from the Anunnaki. When asked tell the people that because Enlil is angered by your master Ea you have been banished to South Africa and are building the boat to transport you and your household. Noah did as he was told. When the floods came the Anunnaki who remained on Earth evacuated to their spacecraft and Noah and his family entered and sealed the submarine. Ea sent his navigator along with Noah. Ninmah and Inanna, (Enlil's granddaughter on Earth born) cried out. From the spacecraft they could see the devastation on Earth. After the immense tidal wave swept over the Earth the skies opened and for seven days it rained. When the wall of water reached it's limits the onslaught ceased but it rained for another forty days. When the rained stopped there was no dry land. The Anunnaki in the heavens waited for the flood waters to recede as did Noah and his family on Earth. Once the dry land appeared on Earth Noah and his family emerged from the submarine and built an alter to Lord Ea for sparing their lives. He set a fire upon the alter and sacrificed a lamb to offer Ea. At that time Enlil and Ea were surveying the damage when Enlil smelled roasting meat. There were survivors!!! When they found the survivors, Enlil's anger knew no bounds. With Noah and his family was Ninagal, Ea's navigator. Enlil was so angry his wished to kill his brother by his own hand! All of mankind he wanted to perish in the great flood. He accused Ea of breaking the oath to which Ea retorted, that he had spoke to the hut wall not

Noah. Then Ea revealed the dream vision he had and the Command that the Creator of All sent through Galzu. When Ninmah heard the news that Noah and his family survived the calamity and that it was by the will of the Creator of All she was pleased as was Ninurta. Ninurta attempted to calm his father down by explaining to his father that it is the will of the Divine Creator that mankind has survived. It was by the will of destiny not fate that the Earthling had been created. Ninmah swore an oath to which Enlil reluctantly agreed, to never repeat the annihilation of Mankind. The Trinity then blessed Noah and his family, be fruitful and replenish the Earth. Now all of the old settlements were buried under mud. All that remained was The Landing Place. After clearing debris and tree braches the evacuated Anunnaki began returning to Earth. Marduk traveled to Mars to assess the damage and found the planet's atmosphere sucked out, waters evaporated, and over taken by dust storms. In South Africa the mines were gone, the city built for smelting and refining the gold was also gone. The multitudes of primitive workers who worked in the city were all gone. On Nibiru the atmosphere was breaching, the need for gold was great. On the other side of Earth pure gold that required no smelting or refining was found. *This was in South America.* High in the mountains, on this side of Earth more survivors were found, descendents of Kain. When the Trinity heard of more survivors they were happy even Enlil was not angered by the news. *Just another thing they neglected to tell us. Noah and his family were not the only ones to survive the Great Flood. Also I believe this is why Hitler claimed to be the superior race. Because he felt that because Noah was a Demigod and chosen by 'God' to save Humanity that the Blond Blue Eyed race was being declared by God as Superior to all others on Earth.* Now new settlements had to be established, regions and domains assigned. A new Landing Place was built, as well as a new mission control center. *It is at this time that the Great Pyramids of Giza and the Sphinx were built. Another great mystery solved. The pyramids were not built by Hebrew slaves but by the Anunnaki. Earth Humans were not allowed to help build the pyramids because of the purpose that the pyramids would serve, the new Mission Control Center. The Anunnaki did not want the Earthling to have access to the Mission Control Center. Now we know why we have not been able to duplicate them even with our current technology.*

Ancient Sumerian Text

Temple of Ziggurat, the alter Noah but to honor Ea for sparing his family's life.

The face on the Sphinx is that of Ea's son Ningishzidda because he was the one who designed it. Once again Marduk felt slighted. Utu, Enlil's son, on Earth born was given command of the Landing Place. Ningishzidda was honored by placing his face on the Sphinx. Marduk went to his father and asked what of the promise that you made to me, that I would rule the Earth? It should be my face on the Sphinx not my brother's. This angered Ningishzidda as well as Marduk's other brothers. Now the clamoring for land and devoted Earthlings began. Ninmah was the one who bought about peace. The Earth and the surviving Earthlings would be divided among the Anunnaki. The descendants of Noah's oldest and youngest son, Shem and Japheth went to dwell in Enlil's domain. Ham went to Ea's domain where Ea made Marduk their master to appease him.

All was completed and the Anunnaki resumed shipping gold to Nibiru. Ninmah was proclaimed Peace Maker. Her domain was in Tilmun (Land of Missiles) in the mountains of Mesopotamia.

Ninmah's Temple

The Great Sphinx, located in Egypt, Ea and Marduk's Domain.

Ancient India, Inanna's Domain

Pyramids in Peru, This was Inanna's Domain.

Pyramids in Nubia, This was Ea's and Marduk's Domain

Chapter Four: The Great War

The next rivalry did not come about because of Marduk, and Ninurta or Ea and Enlil. It was Marduk's sons Asar and Satu. Asar as eldest was successor. Satu's wife and father in law Shamgaz, (the one who convinced soldiers on Mars to take daughters of Adam as wives) plotted to murder Asar so that Satu would become the successor. They got him drunk and placed him in a coffin and threw the coffin in the sea. Asta, Asar's wife went to Marduk seeking revenge and a legal heir. It was decided to allow Satu to live and be the keeper of Asta and to provide her an heir. Asta was not satisfied with this judgment so she decided to extract the life seed from Asar's phallus and impregnate herself. When Satu proclaimed himself sole heir and successor to Marduk, Asta refuted his claim and announced that she was pregnant. She went to the dark hued lands to raise her son in hiding. She named him Horon he was a hero, he would be his father's avenger. In the meantime the rebels from Mars were proliferating and demanding domains of their own. Shamgaz had ambitions to be a great leader. In his heart he coveted Marduk's lands. Horon was adopted by his great uncle Gibil, Marduk's brother who trained and instructed him in the arts of metals. Horon made weapons and formed himself an army of loyal Earthlings and challenged Satu to a one on one battle. Satu shot Horon with a poisoned dart, Satu fell. Asta sent out a cry to heaven and Ningishzidda, came from his spacecraft to save the fallen Horon. He gave him an antidote to the poison and by the morning he was healed. Once again Satu and Horon battled this time Horon was the victor. He took Satu captive and with his uncle Ningishzidda they went before the council. Satu was sentenced to remain blind and heirless; he would die as a mortal with the rebels of Mars. Horon inherited his father's throne. Marduk was pleased with the judgment but still concerned because Horon was by his mother a descendant of Shamgaz. He and his wife were also greatly grieved by the lose of both of their sons. *This is the legend of Horus. These were aerial battles that were fought.* Enlil was observing all that was taking place. He summoned his three sons to a meeting. His main concern was building alternative Mission Control facilities, because the current one was located in Marduk's domain, and an alternative Landing Place. The rebels were causing disruption and breaking all the established rules. They were claiming Mission Control Center theirs by rights of Satu. Horon, an Anunnaki has raised an army of Earthlings and taught them the secrete of making weapons. Ninurta was assigned the task of building these facilities in secrete from the Anunnaki. Ninurta built these facilities in his domain in the mist of trusted Earthlings (descendants of Kain). These facilities were not as sophisticated as those in Marduk's lands but they will serve the purpose. *These are the pyramids in South America. Here we see that the Earthlings were divided among the Anunnaki, and the Earthlings were loyal to their 'God'. The God being, whoever's domain you resided in. This is why in the bible it talks about worshiping false gods, idols, and evil deities. Soon after these events religion would be born. Now what lead to the Great War? A tragic love story, between Enlil's grand daughter, Inanna and Marduk's younger brother Dumuzi.*

Pyramids in South America, Ninurta's Domain,
the alternate facilities built in secrete.

Inanna was a beauty beyond description, and she fell deeply in love with Ea' youngest son Dumuzi. Dumuzi was equally taken with Inanna. Enlil and Ea were greatly pleased by the love that their offspring shared. They both hoped that the union of Inanna and Dumuzi would bring peace to their clans. Every one but Marduk was pleased to here of Dumuzi's betrothal. Marduk was jealous of Dumuzi because since the death of Asar, Ea had favored Dumuzi. Inanna was favored by Enlil as well. Dumuzi was a Shepard and Inanna was a skilled soldier, pilot, and astronaut. As was the custom, Inanna went to her sister in law to have her wedding dress made. While she was visiting with Geshtinanna, she disclosed her vision for the future with her new husband. She would have his name exalted above all other Anunnaki, together the rebellious nations they will subdue, to Dumuzi she would give the status and her hands would direct the nations. Geshtinanna reported all that Inanna told her to Marduk. Marduk was not pleased to hear of Inanna's ambitions and so he and his sister plotted against their brother. The plan was for Geshtinanna to go to Dumuzi and demand he give her a legal heir so that his offspring with Inanna would not be successor to the throne. After he poured his semen into her womb, he had a premonition of his death. He told his sister of his vision and she informed him that Marduk intended to accuse him of rape and have him arrested, in order to disgrace him and end his espousal to Inanna. Fearful for his life, Dumuzi flees to the place of the mighty water falls to hide from Marduk. Dumuzi fell to his death into the waters after slipping on a rock. Ea was greatly distraught to hear this news, he the Master of the Water (The Fish God) has had a grandson and now a son killed by water. Also causing him great distress was that fact that Marduk had instigated the evil plot that had caused the death of his beloved Dumuzi. Because of his actions Marduk too will suffer. Inanna grieved her beloved Dumuzi. She went deep into the Under World to retrieve the remains of her beloved and prepare him for burial. Her sister, guardian of the Under World suspected that Inanna had ulterior motives so at each of the seven gaits she required that Inanna remove a layer of clothing and a weapon until she was naked and with out weapons. When Inanna arrived she killed Inanna. Inanna's father became concerned with the disappearance of Inanna and sent inquiries to Ea as to her whereabouts. Ea fashioned two beings without blood who were unaffected by death rays and sent them to the Under World to retrieve Inanna. When they found her body, they gave to her the Water of Life and the Plant of Life and she arouse from the dead. She ordered them to get the body of Dumuzi, and return to Dumuzi's land. Once there prepare his body for the Day of the Arising. She made her way to Dumuzi's father Ea. She demanded the death of Marduk for the death of her beloved Dumuzi. Ea could not concede. His son was guilty of being an instigator but not of murder. Inanna then went to her parents seeking revenge. *This would be the legend of Isis and Osirus. All Enlil needed was a reason....* Enlil summoned his sons, Inanna, and Utu, Inanna's twin bother to a meeting. Utu informed Enlil of secrete meetings between the rebels and Marduk. They speculated that they may form an allegiance and because of their interbreeding with the Earthlings their armies would be great. They must rid the Earth of the Evil Serpent, Marduk! He demanded that Marduk surrender. Ea felt he must defend his son, Dumuzi died by the hand of ill fate not Marduk's hand. And so the Great War erupted between Enlil's clan and Ea's clan. Inanna started the war and only Marduk's death would satisfy her rage! *These are the battles described in the book of revelation. Could it be another great mystery is revealed? Yes the book of revelation is a book of history not prophecy. Jesus was not even born at the time these events took place, to include the rapture. Any text written by Jesus in the book of revelation was added later by the counsel Nicea. This was the bloodiest war ever fought on Earth, an Anunnaki war in which they recruited Earthlings to build their armies. Biological and nuclear weapons were used during this war. We have been fighting their wars until this very day. Look at the current world stage, the very areas that were at war thousands of years ago are still going on today. After the war the Earth would be divided into four regions.*

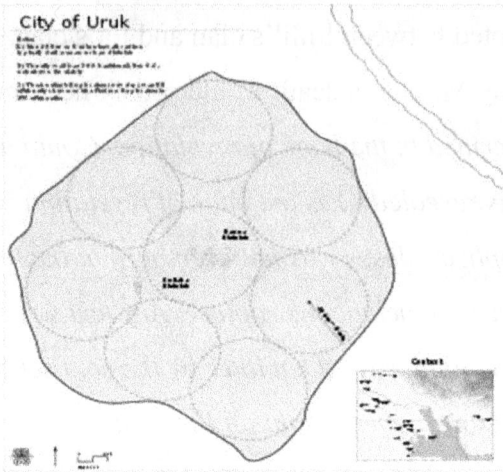

Inanna's Royal city in Sumer

Marduk was buried alive in this Pyramid and later released, at which time the tunnels were made to aid in his escape

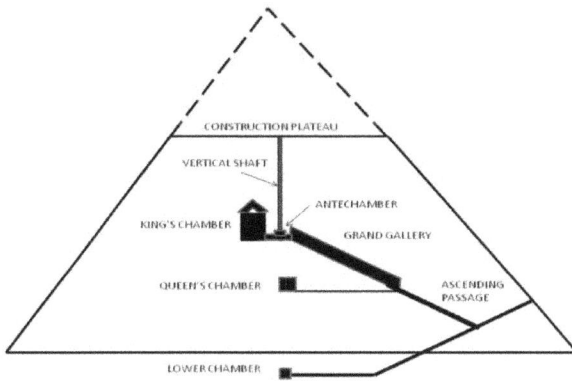

CONSTRUCTION PLATEAU

VERTICAL SHAFT

ANTECHAMBER

KING'S CHAMBER

GRAND GALLERY

QUEEN'S CHAMBER

ASCENDING PASSAGE

LOWER CHAMBER

Enlil's Clan was victorious trapping Marduk in a tunnel of the great Pyramids of Giza. To let Marduk die a slow death by being buried alive satisfied Inanna. *This is the bottomless pit referred to in the book of revelations.* When Marduk's wife heard of his imprisonment and punishment she was deeply distraught. She went to Ea to demand that Marduk be returned to the land of the living. Ea sent her to Utu and Nannar, Inanna's father to see if they would speak to Inanna and plead for Marduk's life. Inanna refused to set Marduk free, he must die for instigating the death of her beloved Dumuzi! Ninmah, the peace maker summoned her brothers and suggested that Marduk be freed under the conditions that he remain in exile and the succession on Earth will now go to Ninurta, all of the heaven and Earth bond facilities be entrusted to Enlil alone, Marduk's lands must be entrusted to another of Ea's sons, and the rebels must give up the landing place. Ea agrees to Enlil's terms, to let Marduk live in exile. Ningishzidda fashioned tunnels in the Great Pyramid to release him. When Marduk heard the conditions of his release he was livid! He would rather die than to give up his birth right! His wife and son, Nabu greeted him and she consoled him by reminding him that they were his future. Angry yet humbled by his wife's words he yielded to fate and he and his family departed to a land of no return, where the horned beast were hunted. Ninurta was named Enlil's surrogate in all the lands on Earth. So the Enlilites won the war. But there remained a problem, The Earthlings now out numbered the Anunnaki on Earth. The rebels and Marduk had interbred with them and now the Anunnaki needed a means by which to separate themselves from the Earthlings and make them obey and serve them. Mankind is allotted three regions, the forth region was allotted for the Anunnaki. Each region was assigned an Anunnaki Leader. Enlil assigned himself the First Region, the Edin. The Second Region, the lands along the Nile and the oceans was assigned to Ea. Inanna was assigned the Third Region, the Indus Valley. The Forth Region, the Sinai Peninsula, was consecrated for the Anunnaki alone. Within each region sacred precincts were established for a priesthood where secrete knowledge would be taught to mankind to worship the Anunnaki as lofty lords.

This is when the greatest enslavement tool was developed, Religion. Once again the Anunnaki set the world stage for war. My god is better than your god. Each god established their laws for their regions and forbade their servants from straying to another region and serving another god. Because of our biological connection to the gods, we still fight their wars over dominions and domination. Marduk was the first to manipulate history. He creates a new religion in which he declares himself 'Supreme God', changes his name to Ra, claims all the attributes of the gods as his alone and changed the name of Nibiru to Marduk. His son Nabu would become his prophet. In his new religion he promises his loyal subjects an after life in the land of the Gods, The Edin. Where he will allow them to drink of the sacred waters of life and they will live forever and become a god. Does that sound familiar? Religion has been used to exploit the human spirit from the beginning. Instead of telling us the entire truth of our story they manipulated the truth in order to enslave our minds. Imagine that!!! We really do live in the Matrix. It is a Matrix of lies that has exploited man kind into wars that have everything and nothing to do with who we are. I have struggled to overstand the whole concept of racism my entire life. In my eyes I only see one race on Earth, the Human race, we have separated ourselves based on cultural and religious differences. Now I understand where it comes from and why we feel it so intensely. The roots of racism can be found in religion. So in order for racism to be eradicated the lies contained in our religions must be eradicated. I don't think I need to spend much time talking about how the creation of religion has done more to keep mankind separated than it has to unite us. The evidence is in the world's current condition. There eventually came a time when the Anunnaki who were able returned to Nibiru and declared to remove themselves from the affairs of man. They would remain only as emissaries of the Divine Creator of All to mankind. But some who were born on Earth and those such as the rebels, Marduk and his descendants, and any other Anunnaki who had bred with Earthlings remained on Earth. They are our ancestors. How many of you are shocked at the possibility of being a descendant of Satan himself? Adam and Eve started the first royal bloodlines. Each of us can trace our family roots back to one of the gods. Now what should be evident regarding our genealogy is that we are in fact One Family, we share many different cultures, but we comprise One race: The Human Race.

Possibly the Ancient Ruins of Enlil's Abode in Lebanon

Chapter Five: Tower of Babel

ME; tiny objects *(possibly microchips or the crystal skulls that have been found in certain sacred places on Earth)* encoded with formulas for all aspects of science and civilization. It was after the Great War, that King Anu decided to visit Earth to see all that had occurred since the great flood. His wife accompanied him on his trip. Once on Earth the Trinity explained to King Anu how the messenger Galzu had told the Trinity that they were unable to return to Nibiru and to save mankind from the flood. The king was confused by this because he had sent no such messenger. And it was untrue that the Trinity were unable to return, a new serum had been developed to reverse the effects of the aging on Earth. Ninmah suggested that Galzu was indeed an emissary of The Divine Creator of All. The Earthling was destined to be created and inherit the Earth. Anu declared from this point on the Anunnaki would serve as teachers to mankind, emissaries of the Divine Creator of All. To preserve and advance the Earthling is now the Anunnaki's mission. Enlil complains to the king that Ea has kept the ME formulas secrete and will not share them with him. The king tells Ea that he must share the knowledge contained in the ME's with the other Anunnaki on Earth and Ea agrees. When the king meets his great grand daughter Inanna, he is very fond of her and he gives to her the royal city that was built for him and his wife, The City of Uruk as well as his airplane.

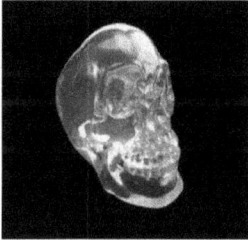

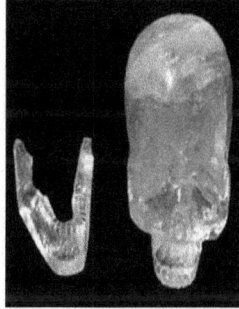

Crystal Skulls

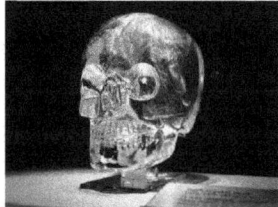

Thirteen crystal skulls of apparently ancient origin have been found in parts of Mexico, Central America and South America, comprising one of the most fascinating subjects of 20th Century archaeology. These skulls, found near the ancient ruins of Mayan and Aztec civilizations (with some evidence linking the skulls with past civilization in Peru) are a mystery as profound as the Pyramids of Egypt, the Nazca Lines of Peru, or Stonehenge. Some of the skulls are believed to be between 5,000 and 36,000 years old.

Many indigenous people speak of their remarkable magical and healing properties, but nobody really knows where they came from or what they were used for.

Were they left behind after the destruction of a previous world, such as Atlantis? Are they simply ingenious modern fakes or can they really enable us to see deeply into the past and predict the future?

Much research is currently being done on the skulls. However, their origin is still a baffling mystery. They seem to defy logic. Everything that is known about lapidary work indicates that the skulls should have been shattered fractured, or fallen apart when carved.

Before his return to Nibiru the king grants Marduk a pardon. He instructs the Trinity to teach mankind the secretes of heaven and Earth, laws of justice and righteousness and then return to Nibiru. Marduk had been exiled for a thousand years. During that time he had lost his wife, now it was just him and his son Nabu that remained. When he heard that Inanna had been given her own region and the king's royal city he was furious. Now came the time to establish the first city of men and select the first king. Ninurta, Enlil's surrogate was selected to establish the center for Civilized Mankind and appoint the first king. He required the ME formulas for kingship. He went to Ea and requested the ME formulas he required and Ea gave them to him. The first city of men, Kishi was a great success. Ninurta taught them all aspects of civilization. Inanna was impatiently awaiting kingship in her region to begin. She decides to steal the ME's from Ea. She got him drunk, convinced him to allow her to hold them and took the ME's while he slept. Ea reported Inanna's evil deed to her grandfather Enlil. Enlil then declared that after the kingship of Kishi was complete kingship would pass to Inanna's domain. This infuriated Marduk. He demanded a sacred city of his own in the Edin. Enlil paid no attention to Marduk's demands. After Marduk's demands go ignored, he decides to build for himself a sacred city. Within the city he planned to build a new landing place. He has his son Nabu summon the rebels from their scattered lands to demand their allegiance and to perform the labor. The rebels and Earthlings out numbered the Anunnaki on Earth at this time and of the Earthlings most were descendants of Ea, who was Marduk's father. And Marduk was the leader of the rebels. So Marduk had the allegiance of at least two thirds of Earth's population. When Enlil heard of Marduk's intentions of building a new landing place and entrusting it to Earthling, he was furious. Enlil summoned his sons and grandchildren to devise a plan to stop Marduk and his evil plan. It was decided to destroy the city and the landing place that they were building with fire and brimstone and to breach the Earthling's unity with confusion by confounding their languages. Their mission was successful and after these events in every region and land the people spoke in a different language. Marduk retreated to his father's domain where he hoped to become master. Upon arriving in his father's domain Marduk discovered that his younger brother, Ningishzidda was ruling. He challenged his brother for ruler ship and his brother refused. For almost four hundred years they quarreled about ruler ship. Until Ea suggested that Ningishzidda concede and depart to other lands for peace sake. Marduk establishes lordship in Ancient Egypt. He replaces his brother's face on the sphinx with that of his son Asar. Marduk becomes Ra and appoints an Earthling as king. Ea gives Marduk all of the ME formulas with the exception of reviving the dead. Ra's region was very successful. When it was time Inanna's royal city, given to her by King Anu, was granted kingship. She appointed her nephew the first king. Now eager to establish the Third Region the leaders decreed it along with Ninmah's authority to Inanna. But Ea refused to give Inanna the ME formulas for civilization because of the ones the she stole for her royal city. He told her to share those with the Third region. Because of this in The Third Region civilized mankind did not fully blossom. *Will the drama ever end? Now up until this point I have not mentioned a particular group of Anunnaki. These are the Mothers of Man and the Daughters of Ma. When it was decided to create the primitive worker, it was Ninmah and Ningishzidda who actually performed the creation. Ninmah was the first Anunnaki to give birth to the primitive worker. She gave birth to twins, one male and one female. Remember the purpose of their creation, to proliferate and take over the work in the mines. After Ninmah successfully gave birth to the first Earthlings, she requested that seven of her nurses volunteer to do the same. Ea's wife was among the nurses who volunteered. These women gave birth to Us and would become the guardians of Us. These women come from all sects of society and from all families, Anunnaki and Earthling. united they form a powerful sisterhood and a powerful military force. They are learned in biology, martial arts, warfare, healing, magic, astrology, and wisdom. They are known by some as DOMA, Daughters of MA. Were it not for Inanna's allegiance to these women, she would have lost the Great War. Ninmah was the leader of these women on Earth. So when Inanna was granted Ninmah's authority, her authority became almost greater than her grandfather's on Earth. If you had to go to war, you wanted Inanna on your team. War was never too far away where Inanna's and Marduk's ambitions were concerned.*

Inanna's Temple in her Royal city.

Ancient Aircraft

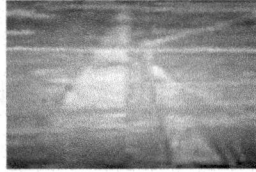

Ancient Landing Sites

Chapter Six: Sodom and Gomorra

Now Inanna still mourned her beloved Dumuzi and coveted the lands the he would have inherited had he not been killed because of his brother's treachery. Marduk, who as far as Inanna was concerned, should be dying a slow death locked away in the pyramid, instead he was ruling the lands that should be hers. And to top it off his lands were more successful than hers because his father had given him all the ME's. In a dream vision, Dumuzi promised her the lands of the two narrows. Inanna came to believe that Dumuzi had been reincarnated, and returned to her. This man's name was Banda, he was of her brother Utu's seed. When she took him to bed and awoke in the morning to find him still alive, she proclaimed herself goddess of immorality. Up until this point any man that she took to bed died in his sleep. *(talk about poison)* Banda was appointed king in Inanna's Royal City. He took for his wife, an Enlilite, Ninsun. Their son was the hero Gilgamesh. Gilgamesh longed to know the secrete of long life bestowed upon the gods. His mother pleaded with Utu to take him to the landing place until he agreed. Ea fashioned for him a being without blood, like the ones he sent to the underworld to retrieve Inanna, to travel with Gilgamesh as a guide and protector. Once they found the secrete tunnels that lead to the Anunnaki cities, they encountered the Bull of Heaven, the Bull of Enlil. The being killed the bull. Gilgamesh continued on his journey. After many adventures along the way he reached the Fourth Region where he meet Noah and Noah revealed the secrete of long life to Gilgamesh. It was a plant. Ea had granted Noah and his wife the gift of long life. That night while Noah slept Gilgamesh uprooted the plant and fled back to the Cities of the gods. But before he arrived a snake was attracted by the plant's fragrance and took the plant while Gilgamesh slept. He returned to the Cities of the Gods where he died a mortal. *So goes the legend of Gilgamesh. And to think back then people were living up to a thousand years. It's not that we are afraid to die, we are dying way too soon and subconsciously we know this. Back in the day we were a lot healthier. We knew how to eat to live. Today we live to eat. We should not eat anything that is dead. When we consume dead meat we are telling our bodies we are ready to die. And of course the body responds to our request, it was designed that way. Drinking the milk of another species is just not natural but we drink it instead of the milk from our mother's breast. We don't want to die, but we are ignorant as to how to live. There will come a time when we will be granted the essence of longevity, but not until we evolve emotionally and spiritually. That may be for some time still.*

*Now let's get back to the story :*Marduk was troubled by Inanna's dream vision and intrigued by the fact that she had proclaimed herself the goddess of immortality. He began to ponder the idea of reincarnation and immortality. The thought of being a god appealed to Marduk. He announced himself as Ra, The Bright One. To ensure the loyalty of his followers he promised them immortality and an after life on Nibiru. He authored a book of secret knowledge that contained the path to take to get to the landing place, and the coordinates to Nibiru, the location of the Plant of Life, the Waters of youth and how the Anunnaki came to be on Earth. He appointed his only surviving son, Nabu as his prophet. He taught that gold was the flesh of the Anunnaki. He invaded his brother's lands to obtain gold. His brothers went to their father to complain of Marduk's actions. Marduk paid no attention to his father's reprimands. He desired to rule all four regions and claim his birthright to rule the Earth. He claimed the attributes of the Trinity and most known gods as his own. The Trinity became very concerned with Marduk's assertions and his blatant rebellion. *And you already know Enlil was way past ready to be rid of Marduk.* It was then decided to unite the First Region under one king. They required a warrior king to take down Marduk. Inanna was entrusted to choose the right man for the job. Inanna chose a man called Arbakad. Enlil appointed him king and built a new crown city to unify the First Region near the first city of man, Kishi. Enlil then gave to Arbakad the secret divine device that enshrines the site for kingship. Full of rage Marduk and his son Nabu made their way to the First Region. In the heart of the Edin Marduk established himself. He claimed to be the sole possessor of the sacred soil. There he built his temple, House of the Utmost God. He named his city The Gateway of the Gods. *Hell hath no fury like Inanna scorned.* She went after Marduk's followers with a vengeance unknown before and the blood of humans flowed like rivers on the Earth. Marduk's brother convinces Marduk to leave the Gateway of the Gods for the sake of it's people. Marduk travels from land to land awaiting the Age of the Ram, the time when the heavens declare his supremacy. He became known in his region from then on as Amun, the Unseen One. Inanna then attempted to seize the Fourth Region with an Earthling army. Infuriated Enlil stops her attempts. *We hear about devil worshipers all the time. There is a religious group of people currently today who call themselves Nubians. They are followers of Nabu. Nabu nor his Father were any more or less evil than the other gods. So call them devil worshiper if you like, but Noah is a descendant of Marduk. Can you see how the wars of yesteryear are still being fought today? In one way or another we are all connected to our ancient ancestors and their ambitions. The wars that are being waged today are the same wars, over the same regions that were being fought in ancient days. Just as in Sodom and Gomorra when nuclear weapons were used, we are facing nuclear warfare today. Who will save us from our impeding fate, or destiny? How can we put a stop to the wars? Where is the voice of reason? Is there one on Earth today worthy of breaking the Seventh Seal? The man who's only agenda is to tell the truth, the man or woman that will stand unafraid for true righteousness and justice. Is there such a person among us?* After Marduk became the Unseen One, chaos ruled the Second Region. In the Fourth Region kingship was transferred from the cities of the gods to the cities of man. It was at about this time when Galzu made another appearance in a dream vision on behalf of the Creator of All. This time he went to see Enlil. He informed Enlil that his time to rule on Earth was coming to an end. That it would soon be the Age of the Ram, replacing the Age of the Bull. Galzu also told Enlil of a coming calamity, just as in the days before the flood a righteous and worthy man would have to be chosen to preserve the Seed of Civilized Man. Marduk was still traveling from land to land with Nabu telling the people of his coming reign and gaining followers along the way. He intended to seize the Fourth Region.

Alliances were formed and wars began to break out in the lands. Enlil observed all that was occurring and was angered. He went to Ea because it was the rulers of his lands that were loyal to Marduk that were invading other lands and demanding submission to Marduk. *300* It was then that Enlil decided it was time to choose the man to preserve mankind's Seed as Galzu had instructed him. But he still did not disclose his dream vision to Ea. He chose Abraham. Abraham was a prince and a priest. He instructed Abraham to protect the sacred places. Once Abraham left for the space port, Marduk arrived in the Fourth Region to find out that Ur-Nammu had appointed himself high priest in the city of Nibru-ki. Marduk assembled the gods and he confessed his transgressions and pleads for his right to rule. He suggests that all the gods submit to his rule and accept his covenant. The Anunnaki are greatly disturbed by Marduk's request for their submission. They were all opposed to Marduk and his son. Ea was the only one to agree to allow Marduk to rule since the oracle has foretold his coming supremacy. Enlil says that if Marduk is to rule then he will not allow him access to the space ports. He decides to use nuclear weapons to destroy the cities where the space ports are located. With the exception of Ea all the Anunnaki agreed to destroy the cities. Ninurta and Nergal, Marduk's brother, were chosen to perform the evil deed. Enlil instructed them to evacuate the cities in an effort to spare lives. It was then that he told Ninurta of his dream vision and told him to warm Abraham of the coming calamity. *Again we are all familiar with the story of Sodom and Gomorra. But as you can see it was not about a city of homosexuals and prostitutes as described in the bible. It was about keeping access to sacred knowledge and locations from the rebellious one.* They destroyed the cities with seven weapons of terror. Once the evil deed was complete Ninurta and Nergal were satisfied that they were successful in depriving Marduk of control of the space ports and sacred secretes that he coveted. What they had not planned on was the evil wind that the nuclear blast caused. They tried to evacuate, the evil wind killed all in it's path. There was no safe place to escape it. The First Region was desolate, The Second region was in confusion, and The Third Region was wounded. The only city that was spared from the nuclear blast was Marduk's city Babili. Because Marduk's city was the only one to survive, Ea told Enlil that it must be the will of the Creator of All that Marduk's time to rule has indeed arrived. To the will of the Creator of All they must submit. It was at that time that Enlil revealed his dream vision to Ea. Enlil accepted Marduk's Victory, agreed give Marduk his allotted rank that had been intended for Ninurta, and he and Ninurta would depart to the Americas. So at long last Marduk was granted the supremacy he sought. Ruler of The Four Regions he was!

Chapter Seven: The Teachers

So Marduk was granted supremacy and all should have been right with the world. You have only to read The Old Testament to know that the wars continued. Now the rivalry was between Marduk and the DOMA. Even though Anu had instructed the Anunnaki to teach mankind and leave many Anunnaki remained in the background of the political, religious, and spiritual affairs of men. The younger generations of the Anunnaki born on Earth were rebellious. Some sought political strength, others saw greater potential in gaining the loyalty of Man in religion, and there were those who sought to obey the Creator of All's will; to teach man the truth of Humanity and Spirituality. From these efforts to teach Man Spirituality came four great teachers or prophets. The one we are most familiar with is Jesus Christ, the second one in none other than the Prophet Mohammad, the third is John the Baptist and last but certainly not least, The Buddha. All but one of these men is believed to have been born of Immaculate Conception. The mothers of all of these men were chosen because they were of royal blood, priestess and loyal to the DOMA. Remember them? Just as in the days of our creation these women volunteered to give birth to these men. They were all test tube babies, lol. Seriously, what we know today as artificial assimilation was the method used to impregnate theses women. Not a miracle, but a scientific procedure. The women who gave birth to our prophets were of the Earth but the Seed with which they were impregnated with was pure Anunnaki. Once these men were born they were taken to the High Temple and taught the Human Story and given all manner of knowledge. When the time came they were sent out into the world to teach Man the Art of being Human as was The Creator of All's will. You have only to read their message to acknowledge that they all came from the same Source. *Is it so hard to believe that different messengers would be sent to different regions at different times to teach? All of them are known world wide.* Because of Inanna's allegiance to the DOMA, she had a powerful military force supporting her. The DOMA had vowed to take on the responsibility of the civilization and education of Man. The intention was to free man from worshipping the Anunnaki and to give him knowledge of The One True God, The Creator of All and eventually invite him into the Human Race not as slaves but as equals. Inanna claims to be the Prophet of the Most High. This did not set well with Marduk and other Anunnaki who had political agendas and had established their religious and political authority on Earth. To free mankind meant to give up their authority and that is the one thing that they were unwilling to do. Marduk unable to defeat the DOMA in military battle went after what they loved most, their children on Earth. The war soon became a battle of the sexes. Women on Earth have suffered the effects of that war until this very day. I wanted to go into more details about the lives of The Teachers but I realize that people hold a very deep connection to these men and the message that they shared. So I will not, other than to say that they all made the ultimate sacrifice for Our freedom. More than deserving of our reverence they are! They never asked us for our worship. With the message that was intended to free us, man has continued to use it to exploit and imprison us. They teach us to pray with our eyes closed, so that should an Emissary of God appear you will not see him. They teach us to pray with our hands closed so that we can not receive the blessing. In hopes of keeping us blind, deaf and dumb. Freedom is our Birth Right!!! 'Emancipate yourself from mental slavery, none but our selves can free our minds'

~Bob Marley~

'The Kingdom of God is within you and all around you, …..Seek and ye shall find, knock and the door shall be opened' ~Jesus of Nazareth~

'All that we are is the result of all that we have thought'.

 ~The Buddha~

'If you're looking for the answer, you gotta ask the question'

~Lauryn Hill~

'Fear will build for you many of prisons, it is the Rage is courage that shall set you free'

~Aye, Daughter of Ma~

Now the time has come to emancipate our selves. To my Sisters of the Earth I say this, you are the greatest creature created and placed on this Earth!!! Man has demonized us thru the use and manipulation of religion and because of his physical strength he has dominated and subjugated us. We have a powerful force of Star Sisters who will help us reclaim our rightful place in the Human Race. We will no longer remain beneath the man as he would have us remain. We will take our rightful place in the forefront and set the example of true righteousness and justice.

Is what I say in this book so hard to believe? The Mayan calendar ends in the year 2012. Could it be that Nibiru is near? Have you seen it? It has been in plain view for the last year that I am aware of. The Anunnaki swore an oath never to allow mankind to be annihilated again, so I can only assume that as this cycle is coming to an end perhaps they will reveal themselves to us in order to prepare us for the coming calamity. Our governments are well aware of their existence and influence in our societies. UFO's for the most part do not come from our skies, they are actually SFOs, submerged flying objects. They come from our oceans, where I believe some of the Anunnaki hide their presence from us on Earth. I believe there are other locations on Earth where they hang out. The Bermuda Triangle, I believe is the gateway, or star gate if you will. The mountains, the oceans, and other remote locations on Earth where we rarely venture into are where they hang out. The time has come to re-examine the teaching of these great teachers and see in them the True meaning of being Human as they were intended, to at long last combine the messages that they sacrificed their lives to bring us. The message of the power of One. 'Children of the Books if you all would put half the energy into understanding one another, as you do in proving the other's belief false, then perhaps the task at hand would be that much easier.'

~Ma Di~

Consider for a moment that 2012 will not bring the end of the world, but an intergalactic family reunion.

Marduk I Ain't Mad At You

Son of the Artful Fashioner you are,

Leader of the Rebels on Mars,

Worshipped in the Ancient Land of Egypt

As the Sun god RA,

Where you honored your father as Ptah.

Your Prince Hood on Nibiru forsaken

For your wife, One you Us you have taken.

The king and master of Earth to be.

This is the vision that you came to see.

But you were constantly denied your right to supremacy.

Weather by fate or destiny.

Envious of Ianna's lover, your very own brother.

So your brother you betrayed, Ianna grieved,

Went to the underworld, her love to retrieve and bury in his grave.

Only your death will satisfy her rage.

The Great War begins…….

You were tried and convicted as an instigator of murder.

Sentenced to be buried alive….

For a thousand years did you remain.

During that time did you think of Cain?

Later forgiven and release but forced into exile.

Peace you did not find….

Ianna's Kingdom continued to thrive.

Unsatisfied with what you were allotted.

Now against Ianna you plotted.

The War begins again

We ALL know it is time for it to end.

For far too long we have fought this war….

And very few of us even know what we are fighting for.

Has your time to reign not come and gone?

Come now let's bring the family peace.

Is it really so hard to forgive and forget?

Aye

Spiritual Revolution

The time has come for a spiritual revolution.

The time is at hand to realize that religion sets the foundation

But it is not the solution.

Believing this or that does not bring about salvation.

Instead it has breed hatred among our nations.

War can only destroy and not bring about creation.

Our beliefs have only brought about destruction

Raising governments full of corruption.

The so called great ones of our past, surviving on lies

Killing whom they must to ensure their alibis

The religions they gave birth to is nothing more than a

Watered down version of the truth.

Knowledge stolen, altered and rendered as their very own.

In order that they might deceive you and keep you under control.

This is the Matrix.

Aye

Communication

Where is the communication within human relations?

We no longer communicate,

Now there are only conversations and debates.

How I long for communication,

Words with meaning and inspiration.

Are we communicating or are we conversating?

Simply giving conditioned responses to questions we can't hear.

Using words that have no meaning.

Words exploited by definitions until their true meaning disappears.

Definitions become conditions that control our decisions.

Words and definitions used to serve as a prison.

The foundation, an institution we call religion.

These conditions have us in a state of conversation.

The art of communication seen somehow as over rated.

Conversations have us lost in a Spiritual Matrix.

In order to get un-plugged,

Humanity must end the wars and conceive of ONE LOVE.

This is the Great Human Revelation.

ONE SPIRIT, ONE MIND, ONE GOD,

Knowledge of this is mankind's Salvation

Aye

Anti Christ

Stop trying to re program me

Do not try to delete the original seed

With your lies of what was and what will be

Trying to recreate a book in history

And call it prophecy

I know your deep hidden secret

It is your power, your claim to Glory

So why is it that you are afraid to tell the whole story?

Sold humanity for silver and gold

Persecute all maintained The Way of Old

Claimed Divine Authority

Crucified Christ for heresy

Yet your "Divine Institution" commits heresy every day!

Proclaim yourselves the superior race

Yet you don't appear to see that you have fallen from grace

Blinded by your fame and riches

Preaching and teaching lies

A House divided will not stand

You can not serve two masters

For you will love one and hate the other

The Deceiver has died! In case you didn't know

Repent or be destroyed!

Yes his descendents live

But the age of the Ram Has long been over

Now his spell will be broken

And your "Divine Institution" will fall

Jews, Muslims, Buddhist and Christians

Will no longer separate themselves

We choose no one religion, We choose no one tradition

We choose no one god over the other

We choose The Divine Source of ALL that Was, ALL that Is,

ALL that Will BE!

And here on Earth, We claim that which is ours,

By the Divinity of Adam & Eve and the promise that was made to

their seed

The right to live and rule our planet by the rules of Humanity

Not animal brutality

The Truth will be known to ALL eventually

This is reality, repent now and give birth to peace

The seed is ripe, labor pain will be great

But there is no purer moment of love than when

A mother gives birth!

Aye

One Nation

The things I worry about:
The betrayal of humanity,
My perception being viewed as insanity
Appreciation of my beauty being called vanity
Political corruption, religious seduction, alien abductions,
Environmental destruction, genetic manipulation, the lies
That we are told regarding our creation, hell I guess I worry
About the entire situation.
It took some time but the conspirators were successful in
Reconditioning the human mind, leaving the masses Third Eye Blind
But Have no fear for their time is soon over.
First the indictment, then the conviction, and next the Transition.
They could only delay, not stop this mission.
Like Dr, W.E.B. Dubois, I'm down for the cause,
Unplug the human mind from the matrix of preoccupation
Step forward into the great human emancipation
Let the Earth stand as One Nation.

Sword of God

I walk with the Sword of God as my armor,

To your cross I will give no honor.

It is the sword of blood and knows not Love

Thereby The Son of God,

The Truth it attempted to murder

But the Sword of God would prevail

And send the evil doers to their hell

The Truth to rise again standing strong

In the mist of all manner of Sin

From the end back to the time when it all begun

All manner of man must acknowledge The One

It is no longer acceptable to remain Blind, Deaf and Dumb

Return to The Way, The One we must obey

John, Jesus, and Mohammad from The One did come

Carrying Her sword they did lead

Many religions from these three did come to be

Now the time has come for these religions

To unite and stand as One.

I Am Aye

I am woman

And it is not easy you see

Because all that is depends on me

I am the bearer of seeds

I am the provider of needs

I am the Earth beneath your feet

I am the sky above your head

It is I who wrote the book of the dead

I am the Daughter of Rah

I am the Daughter of Mah

I am the essence of love and the enemy of hate

I am the words of wisdom standing at the city's gate

I am the truth that is enlightenment

I am the strength that holds the covenant

I am the mother of nations

It was I who created this devastation

It is I who gave birth to the holy prophets and appointed the

Anointed ones

It is I who gave them the message of oneness so that you,

My most precious and beloved offspring could over come

wickedness

And yet it is I that man has labeled as the wicked one

Recognize and realize that it is I that stood at his

Almighty side when the Earth project first begun

And it is He who has appointed yes me to be the one

I Am Aye

References

1.   ZECHARIA SITCHIN, ' The Lost Book Of Enki', Foremost Authority on Ancient Sumerian Text.

2.   The Holy Torah

3.   The Holy Quran

4.   The Holy Bible

Illustrations

www.ingramcontent.com/pod-product-compliance
Lightning Source LLC
Chambersburg PA
CBHW072208090426
42740CB00012B/2440